92
LOP   212571

AUTHOR
Hill, Anne E., 1974

TITLE
Jennifer Lopez $19.95

DATE DUE	BORROWER'S NAME	ROOM NUMBER

OCT
JAN
M
M

92
LOP   212571
   Hill, Anne E., 1974-
      Jennifer Lopez

                  $19.95

GALAXY OF SUPERSTARS

Ben Affleck

Backstreet Boys

Brandy

Garth Brooks

Mariah Carey

Matt Damon

Cameron Diaz

Leonardo DiCaprio

Céline Dion

Tom Hanks

Hanson

Jennifer Love Hewitt

Lauryn Hill

Jennifer Lopez

Ricky Martin

Ewan McGregor

Mike Myers

'N Sync

LeAnn Rimes

Adam Sandler

Britney Spears

Spice Girls

Jonathan Taylor Thomas

Venus Williams

CHELSEA HOUSE PUBLISHERS

GALAXY OF SUPERSTARS

Jennifer Lopez

Anne E. Hill

CHELSEA HOUSE PUBLISHERS
Philadelphia

Dedication: *For my brother, John (JAM). May all your musical dreams come true.*

Frontis: *As an actress and singer who draws thousands of fans from all ethnic backgrounds, 29-year-old Jennifer Lopez is breaking ground for Latino artists in the United States.*

Produced by
21st Century Publishing and Communications, Inc.
New York, New York
http://www.21cpc.com

CHELSEA HOUSE PUBLISHERS

Editor in Chief: Stephen Reginald
Managing Editor: James D. Gallagher
Production Manager: Pamela Loos
Art Director: Sara Davis
Director of Photography: Judy L. Hasday
Senior Production Editor: J. Christopher Higgins
Publishing Coordinator/Project Editor: James McAvoy

The Chelsea House World Wide Web address is
http://www.chelseahouse.com

First Printing

1 3 5 7 9 8 6 4 2

Library of Congress Cataloging-in-Publication Data

Hill, Anne E., 1974–
    Jennifer Lopez / Anne E. Hill.
        p. cm. — (Galaxy of superstars)
    Includes bibliographical references and index.
    Summary: A biography of Jennifer Lopez whose determination has led to success as an actress and singer.
        ISBN 0-7910-5775-5 — ISBN 0-7910-5776-3 (pbk.)
    1. Lopez, Jennifer, 1970– —Juvenile literature. 2. Actors—United States—Biography—Juvenile literature. 3. Singers—United States—Biography—Juvenile literature. [1. Lopez, Jennifer, 1970– . 2. Actors and actresses. 3. Singers. 4. Women—Biography. 5. Hispanic Americans—Biography.] I. Title. II. Series.

PN2287.L634 H55 2000
791.43'028'092—dc21
[B]   99-462032
                                                                            CIP
                                                                             AC

Contents

BILLBOARD'S
TOP SPOT

The buzz in Hollywood in the spring of 1999 was deafening. Everyone wanted to know: Was actress Jennifer Lopez really recording an album? Fans were thrilled, and critics were skeptical. Nevertheless, the diva of the film world was about to take the music industry by storm.

Jennifer always wanted to sing. At 28 years old, she was the highest paid Latina actress in movie history—earning a reported $2 million for her role in 1998's *Out of Sight*. Jennifer was both proud and happy of what she had accomplished. But she still felt like there was something missing. Never one to let a dream go unfulfilled, Jennifer convinced the most talented people in the music industry to help her record a CD.

Not long after that, Jennifer's musical dreams came true. In June 1999 the first single from her debut album, *On the 6*, went to number one on the *Billboard* charts. "If You Had My Love" replaced a single by another Latino artist, pop phenomenon Ricky Martin. "Yeah, it's No. 1 on the *Billboard*. Excuse me, it's No. 1 on the *Billboard* charts. I'm so excited I can't even talk," she said.

To the surprise of some music critics, Jennifer's debut album, On the 6, *went platinum in less than eight weeks, and her single "If You Had My Love" reached number one on the* Billboard *charts.*

For the first time, Jennifer was getting requests to perform her music rather than answer questions about upcoming films. She sang at the MTV Movie Awards and appeared on television shows like *The Rosie O'Donnell Show*, *The Oprah Winfrey Show*, and *The Tonight Show with Jay Leno.*

Still, many interviewers asked the same question: why had she chosen acting if singing was her true love? The ambitious young woman had an answer. "You know I started my career singing and dancing, doing musical theater and stuff like that which a lot of people don't know. So it was always part of the package for me, singing, dancing, acting, it was always the pursuit of a career for me, it was the three things," she explained. "So you know I just went from there. It's kind of like where my career kind of took me. I just followed the path that was in front of me, and it just worked out that the acting took off first."

Ironically, Jennifer's breakout role as an actress was her portrayal of Tejano singer Selena, the 23-year-old sensation who was murdered by the president of her own fan club in March 1995. After winning the part from over 20,000 young hopefuls, Jennifer found herself in front of thousands of screaming extras while filming the movie's opening scene in the Houston Astrodome. Jennifer had requested to sing the songs, but executives decided to use Selena's real voice. As she lip-synched along to the music, Jennifer realized that this was what she wanted—to perform in front of a live crowd. There was only one problem—no one knew the beautiful actress could sing.

After two years and a string of successful hits, including the thriller *Anaconda* and the acclaimed *Out of Sight*, Jennifer felt the time was right to approach the music industry with her as-yet-untapped vocal talent. The normally self-confident woman was admittedly nervous. "I wanted to do a Latin-flavored record long before I even started making movies," she told *US* magazine. Jennifer wanted to work with the best. So she did a Spanish demo tape and sent it to the WORK Group, a division of Sony Music. The executives at Sony called her back soon after, asking if she would sing in English. Jennifer agreed. After all, they had successfully promoted many famous divas, such as Mariah Carey and Celine Dion. She trusted that they knew what they were doing.

They, in turn, had faith in Jennifer's abilities. "When she came to the studio, it was like magic," said Emilio Estefan Jr., music producer and husband of Gloria Estefan. "She could definitely sing. People are going to be surprised."

Aligned with some of the most powerful names in the music industry, Jennifer took a break from movies and spent the end of 1998 and the first half of 1999 writing songs and laying down tracks in the recording studio. "After signing with Sony, I discussed how I wanted the record to sound," she told *Latina* magazine. "I was played many songs by artists ranging from Babyface to Diane Warren, but I felt it was important that my record be less pop and have more urban Latin appeal." She wrote one song, cowrote two others, and recorded a duet with Latin superstar Marc Anthony called "No Me Ames," or "You Must Not Love Me."

During the intense recording time, Jennifer relied on the roller coaster of "heightened emotions" she was feeling—anxiety, nervousness, excitement—to write songs. "This album was

Jennifer, shown here performing during the 1999 Billboard Music Awards, dedicated more than six months to creating her first album.

exciting and scary to make. With every script I read I'm like, 'Is this gonna stretch me? Is it gonna make me a little crazy? 'Cause if it is then I'm doing the right thing.' That's how it was with the album. It was a lot of work," she revealed to *Vibe* magazine. "I can't try to be Whitney [Houston] or Faith [Evans]. I do something different. I have something else to offer anybody who'll want to . . . get down."

After working many long days and nights, Jennifer showed WORK how committed she

Jennifer's popularity led to comparisons with Ricky Martin, whose fall 1999 concerts sold out in record time.

was to music. The result was a blend of various musical styles: Latin, hip-hop, R&B, and pop. Tommy Mottola, chairman and CEO of Sony Music, was impressed with the music's effect and all of Jennifer's hard work. "Jennifer has tremendous attitude—and I say that in a positive way—and it comes across onscreen and in person, and she puts that into her singing. . . . Her kind of success doesn't come easy."

Despite all of the effort, Jennifer felt like someone was smiling down on her when her album's release on June 1, 1999, coincided with a new American boom in Latin music. Record executives had noticed growth in the Latin population in terms of numbers, buying power, and devotion to their favorite performers. Latin music sales went from $490.6 million in 1997 to $570.9 million in 1998. "Music has a stronger connection with Hispanics than with other groups," Cary Davis, general manager for La Mega, a radio station in New York, told *Time*. "In a sense you have a double hit with Hispanics: it's good music but it also takes you back to your culture."

Not everyone loved Jennifer's debut album. Some critics had harsh words. *Entertainment Weekly* called her a "Mild Spice Girl." "As soon as Jennifer opens her mouth . . . the husky-voiced voluptuousness that has become [her] trademark in films like *Out of Sight* simply vanishes. Her voice is higher and thinner than expected—not embarrassing, but sadly ordinary." The review did not deter fans from buying both the single and the album, though. Jennifer's popularity, combined with her album sales, led to comparisons with Ricky Martin.

Ricky Martin's arrival on the American music scene had fueled a thirst for more Latin music. Tickets to Martin's fall 1999 concerts sold out in record time, snatched up by fans willing to wait in line for hours and, in some cases, spend hundreds of dollars to see their idol. "It's like a sleeping giant waking up all over the world," Estefan told *Time*. Jennifer commented, "Everything happens for a reason. I mean the fact that the album is coming out at a time [when Latin music is in vogue] is just God telling me, 'Don't worry so much, everything is going to work out OK.'"

Even the name of Jennifer's CD was inspired. The No. 6 train was the line that Jennifer took from the neighborhood where she grew up in The Bronx into Manhattan for dance classes and later on to visit night clubs. "[Manhattan] was a place where dreams were made, you know? Whereas The Bronx was just where you lived. I named my album *On the 6* 'cause that's how I got where I was going, but it was also how I got home."

2

"Fly Girl"

Home for Jennifer was The Bronx, New York, a working-class neighborhood in one of New York City's five boroughs. But the Lopez family's roots are in Ponce, Puerto Rico, where Jennifer's mother, Guadalupe, and father, David Lopez, were born. The two married and moved to the United States, where they had three daughters. Their oldest, born in 1968, was named Leslie. The youngest, Lynda, was born in 1971.

Middle child Jennifer was born on July 24, 1970, a sultry summer day in the city. While the family she was born into was not wealthy, young Jennifer never felt underprivileged in "el barrio," which is Spanish for the neighborhood. There were many other Puerto Rican families nearby, and Jennifer remembers feeling aware and proud of her Latino heritage from the start.

She credits her culture, which has always loved music and dancing, in bringing out the entertainer in her at a very young age. Although neither parent was involved in entertainment—David is a computer specialist for an insurance company and Guadalupe, a kindergarten teacher—Jennifer

From a young age, Jennifer absorbed her Puerto Rican heritage, learning traditional dances such as the Bomba, show here. She credits her culture with bringing out the entertainer in her.

knew she wanted to be a star at age five. "Growing up all I ever wanted to be was a singer and a dancer," Jennifer recalled.

It didn't take long for Jennifer's parents to realize her talent. "She always loved to sing, but she was also a born actress. I always knew that Jennifer would have a great future. Ever since she was a little girl she was acting, living in her own world," Guadalupe remembered. "I know that she is going to combine all of her talents successfully. She is a very special person."

To give Jennifer the opportunity to explore her talents, her parents enrolled her in dance classes when she was seven years old. Lessons in ballet, jazz, piano, and theater soon followed. But schoolwork always came first in the Lopez household. Jennifer and her sisters attended the Holy Family School. While studying at the private Catholic school, Jennifer developed a deep sense of faith and a firm belief in God. This faith would help her later on, when fame and fortune presented her with new challenges. "God is a very big part of my life. I went to Catholic school for 12 years, so I pray a lot: 'Lord, move me in the right direction, give me courage.' I can only do so much, but I know that I'm being guided."

Jennifer also discovered life outside of her small neighborhood. She and her mother would visit her father in Manhattan. "We'd get dressed up, take the train all the way downtown, have lunch, walk around Union Square. We had a whole ritual. It was incredible, seeing things and people and stores we never saw." Living so close to one of the entertainment centers of the world opened up Jennifer's eyes to the possibilities of a career as a performer.

In addition to her schoolwork and performing

Jennifer's parents supported her dreams by providing lessons in ballet, jazz, piano, and theater. She is pictured here with her father, who she says always made her feel pretty.

aspirations, Jennifer had a love of sports. She was a gymnast, competed nationally in track, and was on the school softball team. But it wasn't long before her desire to be a star overshadowed her other pastimes. She acted in community and school productions of musicals such as *Jesus Christ Superstar* and *Oklahoma*.

Pictures of stars like the members of Menudo and Rob Lowe plastered the walls of the small bedroom Jennifer shared with her sisters. Little did the young girl realize that she would one day befriend Ricky Martin, one of the members of Menudo. Jennifer also recruited her sisters to act out scenes from their favorite television show, *Charlie's Angels*. Sounds of all kinds of music—Top 40, Broadway tunes, and Latin—came from their busy bedroom.

Soon, Jennifer discovered hip-hop music. The first time she heard the Sugarhill Gang's "Rapper's Delight" at age eight, she was hooked. "I was an instant fan—the beat of it and the rapping. I would hear that at school and pop and salsa music at home." She later credited all of these types of music with helping her to create her own unique sound.

Hip-hop music and trends also influenced the way Jennifer dressed as a teenager. She donned tight jeans and boots and later dressed like her idol, Madonna. The young woman began developing her now-famous curves, and men's attentions soon followed. "[I'd be] walking down the street and they'd say something—you know how Spanish men are. You're just a little girl and you're like, 'How come they always say it after I pass by?' At first, I hated it, but as I got older, I realized it was a good thing."

Her parents, however, made sure that each of their daughters knew the rules. They taught the girls to stay free of drinking and drugs and about refraining from sex until they were married. "I never had a wild phase," Jennifer recalled. Even now, she claims her late nights are never filled with the usual raucous Hollywood behavior. If she's out late, it's because she's dancing at clubs. Jennifer also insists that she hasn't dated all of the men she's been linked to in the press.

In high school, Jennifer almost gave up her dreams of becoming a performer. "When I was

young, there were some messages I got about what I could and could not achieve because of where I came from." The teen thought about becoming a hairstylist. But after giving her sisters a few bad perms, Jennifer decided to stick with her real dream, no matter what anyone said.

Unfortunately, there were not many Latin role models for Jennifer to follow. She admired performer Rita Moreno and dreamed of playing Maria in *West Side Story*. In fact, she watched the Hollywood classic more than a hundred times. At night, Jennifer and her girlfriends would hit the clubs in Manhattan, like the Palladium and the Danceteria, taking the No. 6 train back and forth.

As graduation day neared in the spring of

Latina actress Rita Moreno, shown here singing and dancing in West Side Story, *was one of Jennifer's role models.*

1987, Jennifer made an important decision—she was not going to college. Her best friend, Arlene, who is her personal assistant today, was not surprised. Nor was Jennifer's boyfriend at the time, David Cruz. They knew that the teen was determined to be a star.

The news was devastating to her parents, however, who had hopes that Jennifer would become a lawyer. David and Guadalupe wanted to be supportive of their daughter's dreams, but they didn't want Jennifer to give up her education. "They thought it was really stupid to go off and try to be a movie star. No Latinas did that—it was just this stupid, foolish crapshoot idea to my parents and to everybody who knew me. It was a fight from the beginning."

That summer, the normally happy and peaceful Lopez household was full of conflict. Jennifer continued to dance and started going on auditions for jobs, but the arguments at home escalated. After one heated battle with her parents, Jennifer stormed out of the house and moved into the Manhattan dance studio where she was training, determined to follow her dreams. "I didn't know what was going to happen, but I knew I would die trying," she later recalled.

Eventually, Jennifer got an apartment with some friends in a tough New York City neighborhood called Hell's Kitchen. As she struggled to make ends meet, the bright lights of Broadway seemed a very long way from her tiny apartment. She recalled times when she was literally down to her last dollar. While the situation was far from ideal, looking back, Jennifer is glad that she chose not to resort to desperate measures to make money, like some young women she knew who were taking their clothes off at strip clubs for a living.

Before long, Jennifer's love of hip-hop music helped her land jobs. "Hammer came out with 'U Can't Touch This,' and all the auditions started becoming hip-hop auditions. I was good at it, and they were like. 'Ooh, a light-skinned girl who can do that. Great, let's hire her!" Jennifer recalled. The trend led to more jobs, and finally she landed a five-month gig dancing on the European tour of *Golden Musicals of Broadway*. Next Jennifer joined a Japanese tour of the theater production *Synchronicity*. In between, she took jobs dancing in music videos.

Almost three years had passed since Jennifer's high school graduation, and her parents had become more accepting of her career choice. The 20-year-old was also pleased with the progress she was making as a dancer and decided it was time to try to break into acting too.

Not long after she made this decision, in 1991, Jennifer was selected from over 2,000 contestants to appear as a "Fly Girl," one of the dancers on the FOX-TV show *In Living Color*. While flattered with the offer and very tempted by the steady money, Jennifer was unsure about what to do. Should she take this offer and remain a dancer or turn it down to try acting? She decided to take the job but expressed her fears to the show's star and producer, Keenan Ivory Wayans. She was grateful for his advice to stick around for two seasons. "He said, 'You'll have money and more experience.'"

While on the set, Jennifer met some people who were important in the entertainment industry. One of them, Eric Gold, the coproducer of the show, later became her manager.

Keenan Ivory Wayans, star and producer of In Living Color, *recommended that Jennifer stay with the show for a couple of seasons, advice she was grateful she took.*

"There was just an unshakable confidence about Jennifer. No doubt, no fear. The girl just had it," Gold later recalled.

The young dancer left New York and moved to Los Angeles, where the TV show was taped. Jennifer always assumed the move would not be permanent, but she has stayed since and now has homes on both coasts. In addition to dancing, Jennifer was already preparing for future film roles by taking speech classes to rid herself of her accent from The Bronx.

The independent-minded New York native had a hard time getting used to taking directions from the choreographer of *In Living Color*, Rosie Perez. An actress and dancer herself, Rosie was extremely demanding, and Jennifer didn't respond well to Perez's direction. Soon, the two were clashing on the set and having heated arguments. Jennifer felt she was being unfairly singled out, while Perez may have seen more talent in the 21-year-old hopeful and pushed her harder than the others. The two eventually worked out their differences and even became good friends.

Later, Jennifer claimed she never really cared about the Fly Girls because what she really wanted to do was act. All she needed was the opportunity, which turned out to be right in front of her.

3

BREAKING IN

Dancing on *In Living Color* was great exposure for Jennifer. Although she was never contacted for any acting roles, the 23-year-old was ecstatic when she learned she had been selected to tour as a dancer with singer Janet Jackson. It was the end of Jennifer's second season with *In Living Color,* and she was ready to move on.

Meanwhile, a producer, who was married to one of the other Fly Girls, thought Jennifer was right for his new FOX-TV series, *South Central.* He asked her to audition for the show, and Jennifer decided it couldn't hurt to try for the part. She was relaxed going in for the reading, knowing she already had a secure job dancing on Janet Jackson's tour. When she learned the part of Lucy was hers, Jennifer faced another tough decision.

The weekend before Janet's tour was set to start, Jennifer made up her mind—she would begin her acting career. She called Janet Jackson's office to decline the offer to tour as a dancer. "The Janet tour is a major job for a dancer," Jennifer's dance coach told *Vibe* magazine. "It's a year and a half of work. But she knew. Other dancers,

---

Jennifer's role as the young Maria in My Family *was just one of many opportunities she took as she sought to break into the movie business.*

they say they want to do this and that, but they never leave [dancing]. Jennifer was just certain." Jennifer knew she had to go for her dream. "I would have literally just died if I didn't go for it," Jennifer said.

Due to poor ratings, however, *South Central* only lasted for one season. During that season Jennifer learned a lot about acting and the long hours that go into producing a television drama. Although the show was short-lived, she had another credit to add to her resumé. Not long thereafter, Jennifer auditioned for and was cast in the CBS series *Second Chances*, starring Connie Sellecca and Megan Follows. Although this series was also short-lived and only aired for one season, Jennifer's character, Melinda Lopez, was so popular, Jennifer was soon playing her on a second series, *Hotel Malibu.*

Jennifer might have been crushed by the string of unsuccessful shows, but opportunities always seemed to present themselves at the right time. Although unable to tour with Janet Jackson, Jennifer did appear in Jackson's hit video *That's the Way Love Goes* and had a part in the made-for-television movie, *Nurses on the Line: The Flight of Crash 7.*

Her move to Los Angeles hadn't been easy, but it looked to be paying off. Jennifer was finally a working actress. Her longtime boyfriend, David, had even moved in with her and taken a job as a movie production assistant. Together, they got a cocker spaniel, whom they named Boots, and David shared in Jennifer's joy when she got a role in her first feature film, *My Family/Mi Familia*, starring Jimmy Smits.

The story focuses on the difficult struggle of a Mexican family immigrating to the United States. It tells the saga of three generations, beginning in the 1920s and continuing through the 1990s. Jennifer played a young woman named Maria, who is one of the central figures in the plot. In the story's beginning, Maria marries Jose Sanchez, a man who has immigrated to California from his native Mexico, and the couple have two children. When she is pregnant with their third child, Maria is shipped back to Mexico by U.S. government troops. For the rest of the film, she fights to get back to the family she was forced to leave.

Playing the young Maria was a challenge, both mentally and physically. In one scene Jennifer had to act in freezing cold water. Acclaimed director Gregory Nava admired the actress's work ethic. "She got right into that freezing water every day for three days and came through without ever complaining. Few actresses would be that heroic and courageous. She's going to be a big star." Nava knew he was right about his find when he saw her on film. "The camera absolutely loves her. She has that true movie-star quality that you hear people talk about."

While Nava's prediction would turn out to be true, Jennifer was just glad to be working. "Breaking in is the hardest part. I've been lucky because I got kinda picked out," Jennifer confided. At 25, Jennifer had worked hard for the recognition she finally attained, and her ambition kept her going when times were tough. What she hadn't counted on was all of the attention she would receive onscreen in her next role.

Released in 1995, *Money Train* starred Woody Harrelson and Wesley Snipes as foster brothers and cops. Jennifer plays undercover cop Grace Santiago, the seductress who causes the guys

Jennifer was also thrilled with the results because of her own input on the album. She recalled:

"If You Had My Love" was produced by Rodney Jerkins. And it's funny, that song when I first got it . . . was a little bit angrier. . . . The lyrics were like, "If you had my love and you said you would do this for me and do that for me," and I was like, No, no, why don't we switch it around a little bit. I'm not an angry person, I'm not really that bitter about love. I'm very optimistic. . . . Why don't we put it more in the context of "If you had my love and I gave it to you, would you do the right thing?" So we switched it around, so I really love it, I really think it's a good song.

The success of the single helped make the album go platinum, selling more than one million copies in less than eight weeks. Jennifer, who was just starting to become a well-known face on the screen, was now a video star. MTV handled requests for the video of the song, which also featured Jennifer's dancing ability and an interactive voyeuristic style. *If You Had My Love* became one of the most popular videos of the summer of '99.

The song was especially popular with teens. In August 1999, they voted "If You Had My Love" the Song of the Summer at the first annual Teen Choice Awards. Dressed in a clingy, copper gown, Jennifer thanked her fans for their support as she clutched her first award for her debut album. A few weeks later she attended the MTV Music Video Awards, where she was nominated in four categories, including Best Dance Video and Best Female Video.

Playing undercover cop Grace Santiago in the 1995 movie Money Train *taught Jennifer how much influence entertainment could have over other people.*

to compete for her affection. Although the role was not written for a Latina actress, Jennifer convinced the director that she was right for the part.

Once she knew the role was hers, Jennifer began researching the lives of transit cops and talking to female police officers about their work. Her extra attention to detail paid off in the end, and Jennifer decided from then on she would always research every part she played.

One thing she couldn't prepare for, however,

was her explicit love scene with Wesley Snipes. While Jennifer was very comfortable with her costar, she worried about her parents' reaction to the scene. There she was acting out the kind of behavior of which her parents had never approved. She was so concerned about the scene, she went home after shooting was over. "I needed the comfort," she explained.

Her mom, accompanied by daughter Lynda, admitted to having a hard time watching the scene at the premiere of the film. But she was proud of her daughter's acting skills. The director, Joseph Ruben, was also impressed with Jennifer. "She's as beautiful as a model, but she can act. You believe she can hold her own on the street."

Jennifer also surprised everyone on the set with her knowledge of guns. Snipes and Harrelson were toting 9-mm guns, while her character carried a .38 revolver. "A .38 is such a girl gun. I'm not gonna carry some sissy revolver," Jennifer said of her character. She knew the violence in the film was fictional, but just days after the film's November 22, 1995, opening, Jennifer realized how films could impact the public.

In a controversial scene in the film, a pyro-maniac squirts flammable liquid into subway token booths and ignites them. On November 26, a clerk in a Brooklyn, New York, subway station was attacked the same way and suf-fered life-threatening burns. There was another attempt at a different station soon after, but the results of the second attack were not as serious. Even though, thereafter, subway patrols were increased and booths equipped with flame-smothering devices, everyone was still shaken by the horrendous violence. Senate Majority

Workers dismantle a firebombed token booth at a subway station in Brooklyn, New York. The crime mimicked a plotline in Money Train *and made Jennifer face hard questions about her work.*

Leader Bob Dole, a longtime advocate of Hollywood morality, even urged people to boycott *The Money Train.*

"It's a terrible crime and our hearts go out to the victims," Jennifer told *People* magazine. But she was also puzzled as to why, with all the violence in the movies, *The Money Train* was being singled out for criticism. "In a way . . . you think the film is responsible, but it's not. It's the [criminals]," she insisted. However, she learned a lesson from the ordeal: "It just made me more conscious of what I do in other movies," she said. "You have such an influence over other people, it's kind of scary."

Jennifer was glad her next project was not an action film. She had been cast by legendary director Francis Ford Coppola in the tender flick *Jack.* Jennifer was thrilled to be cast in the film, especially since her part was not meant to be played by a Latina. The role was originally written as a 35-year-old white woman named Miss Wargo. But executives decided to change the part once Jennifer read for the role. She beat out actresses Lauren Holly and Ashley Judd to play the teacher opposite Robin Williams's character, Jack, a 10-year-old boy who is growing four times faster than normal. As a result, Jack looks 40 but acts his age. Like most 10-year-old boys, when Jack meets his beautiful teacher, he develops a crush on her.

Jennifer knew exactly who to turn to for advice on playing a teacher—both her mom and her older sister, Leslie, are educators. Jennifer wanted to impress Williams, and she especially wanted to do well for Coppola, who is known to be very intense during filming. However, *Jack* was a very different kind of project for the director of such dramas as *The Godfather* trilogy and *Apocalypse Now*. Coppola decided to shoot the entire movie in and around his home in Napa Valley, California. Consequently, shooting was much more relaxed than usual. The experience was one Jennifer would never forget, thanks in part to Coppola. "He's like a big teddy bear, he's so sweet. I would just, like, sit by his feet in between takes and we would watch the monitor. He creates a very nurturing atmosphere."

While Coppola was soothing, Robin Williams provided the entertainment. The actor and comedian played jokes and amazed the cast and crew with his famous impersonations. He even urged Jennifer to join in. Soon the two were amusing everyone on the set with a scene from *Romeo and Juliet*. Williams imitated the voice of a tough action star—Sylvester Stallone—portraying the tender Romeo. Jennifer played Juliet imitating the speech of her former choreographer, Rosie Perez, whose voice is known for its high pitch and squeakiness.

It may have been fun and games on the set, but Jennifer's life at home was another matter. She and David had been dating for 10 years, and the two often discussed getting married. But Jennifer kept stalling, saying that she wanted to be at a certain place in her professional life before she made such a big step in her personal one. David was getting tired of her excuses and her relentless ambition. He was also jealous of Jennifer's love scenes with handsome actors. "Sometimes he got insecure because I did love scenes with powerful men who made lots of money. But it was my job to make it look as if that man were the only one in my life, and I tried to do that," the aspiring actress later revealed to *Latina* magazine.

To make matters worse, Guadalupe disapproved of the relationship. She believed that a woman shouldn't live with a man until after they were married, but she knew better than to interfere in her headstrong daughter's life. She had done that once already, and a furious Jennifer had left home.

In March 1996, Jennifer and David broke up. David moved back to New York City to open a dry cleaning business while Jennifer stayed in Los Angeles. She hadn't been alone in a very long time. However, she felt this provided an opportunity for her to turn all of her attention to her career. The filming of *Jack* was completed, and Jennifer was pleased with her dramatic work. Unfortunately, *Jack* did not do well at the box office. That did not stop Jennifer, who

already had moved on to her next project, the suspense drama _Blood and Wine_.

Once again, she was working with Hollywood heavyweights. Director Bob Rafelson assembled experienced actors Jack Nicholson, Judy Davis, and Michael Caine, along with relative newcomers Stephen Dorff and Jennifer. The film focuses on Nicholson's character, Alex, who is a proprietor of a wine shop in an unhappy marriage. He begins having an affair with Gabriella (played by Jennifer), the Cuban nanny of one of his customers. Alex enlists Gabriella and ex-con Victor (played by Michael Caine) to help steal a valuable diamond necklace from Gabriella's employer. While their scheme doesn't go as planned, Gabriella also finds herself

Although the movie Jack _did not do well at the box office, Jennifer thoroughly enjoyed working with Robin Williams._

Jennifer was relieved that she got along with Oscar-winning actor Jack Nicholson during the filming of Blood and Wine. *She also related strongly to the movie's story line of an immigrant family's struggles.*

falling for Alex's stepson, Jason (Stephen Dorff). She stays with Alex, though, because his wealth and prestige can help her struggling immigrant family. She chooses money over love.

Jennifer strongly identified with Gabriella and her struggles. Jennifer's own parents had been immigrants who worked very hard to make a good life in America. As in several of her other roles, Jennifer had some steamy love scenes. This time they were with the much older and hugely respected Nicholson. Luckily, the two hit it off right away. "Jack and I got along great. He was all into, you know, I was too young for him. I was like, 'No! You can get a chick my age, just not me!' He would look at me and go, 'You are just my kind of dish, I want a girl like you.' But I wasn't giving him a vibe like, 'Oh yeah, we could be together.'"

Instead, Jennifer had her eye on another man. While shooting *Blood and Wine* in Miami, she developed a crush on a waiter at Gloria Estefan's restaurant, Larios on the Beach. After eating there several times, she finally worked up the nerve to introduce herself. Soon, Jennifer and 23-year-old Ojani Noa were inseparable. They were both ambitious—Ojani had aspirations of becoming an actor as well and was already modeling on a part-time basis. Although Jennifer was at a more established point in her career, she felt Ojani understood her intense drive. The attractive couple complemented each other well. "[W]hen we met each other, we just kind of knew," Jennifer remembered.

Ojani seemed to be more comfortable than David had been watching Jennifer get cozy on camera with Nicholson. The duo's big love scene was filmed in front of cast and crew but turned out different than originally scripted. "Jack thought it would be sexier if we did a little salsa dancing," Jennifer told *People*. "He had never salsaed before, so I had to teach him. And you know what? He never once stepped on my toes. He's a good dancer." Still, with her extensive dance background, Jennifer admitted, "I had the upper hand."

Indeed, at the end of 1996, Jennifer had the upper hand on both her career and her personal life. But even she couldn't have foreseen that she would soon make history as the highest-paid Latina actress of all-time.

4

PROFESSIONAL AND PERSONAL SUCCESS

In March 1995, Selena Quintanilla Perez, the 23-year-old Tejano singer who was beginning to cross over into mainstream pop, was murdered by the former president of her fan club. Her death shocked and touched millions. Soon after the tragedy, a movie deal on the life of Selena was in the works. Selena's family wanted the movie to focus on Selena's life rather than her tragic death. "I didn't do the movie to exploit my daughter," Selena's father, Abraham, said. "I did it because there's an insatiable desire in the public to know more about her." The Quintanilla family, along with the filmmakers, including director and writer Gregory Nava, conducted a nationwide talent search for the right young woman to portray Selena.

By this time, Jennifer had become an established actress who was being offered roles without auditions. Nava, who had directed Jennifer in *My Family,* suspected she would be perfect to play Selena and asked her to try out for the part . . . along with 22,000 other hopefuls. "Now, I knew that she was about my age and they might be considering me for it. But it wasn't this thing like 'I have to get this part.' I think it wasn't until I auditioned that I really

---

Starring in the title role in Selena *gave Jennifer the breakthrough moment she had worked so hard for and made her the highest paid Latina actress in movie history.*

As she filmed Selena's story, Jennifer focused on mirroring not only Selena's mannerisms but also her love of life.

wanted it. That's when I realized that there was all the dancing and singing, and then I got really excited about it," Jennifer remembered.

After a series of auditions, seven women— four experienced actresses (including Jennifer) and three unknowns—were asked in for a final screen test. Jennifer had to sing and dance for nine minutes and read eight pages of script. "The search for the young woman to play Selena was not a hoax," Nava said. "It was an honest and open search, and an amateur could have gotten the role, but Jennifer was the best person for the part. We needed someone who could act both comedically and dramatically, lip-synch to Selena's songs and dance. Jennifer was the only one who could do all four. What can I say? Jennifer sparkled," he explained. Selena's family agreed that Jennifer was the best actress for the part. When she signed the contract to play Selena, Jennifer became the highest paid Latina actress in history, earning $1 million for the role.

The final decision was announced at a press conference at which Jennifer got to meet the entire Quintanilla family. "We met in a room near where the press conference was going to be held, and I remember a strange feeling going around the room. It was almost surrealistic," Jennifer remembered. "Here was this big press conference for a movie about Selena, but I was getting all the attention. This was all about Selena, but Selena wasn't there."

After the press conference, many Mexican Americans protested a Puerto Rican-American in the role of Selena. Jennifer was saddened by the reaction. "I thought, 'They don't like me!' But then I realized . . . any actress would have been under tremendous scrutiny because of how beloved Selena was and how fresh that wound was." Before filming began in August 1996, when Jennifer was repeatedly asked about the issue by the press, she explained:

> I don't think the actress who played her had to be Mexican-American just because Selena was. Selena and I were both Latinas and both had the common experience of growing up Latina in this country. That was good enough. The important thing is that a Latina played her; I think a non-Latina would have been under too much scrutiny and would have taken away from the film's impact. Besides, when outsiders look at us, and by [us] I mean all Latinos, they don't see Mexican-Americans or Cubans or Puerto Ricans. They say, "She's Spanish," and that's it.

Ultimately, Jennifer decided that she had more in common with Selena than not. They were both close to their families, incredibly ambitious, defiant, full of energy and charisma, and above all, both loved to perform. In fact, these similarities had been the deciding factor in her winning the part. "[W]e were looking for someone who could capture Selena's spirit. She just had it," Nava said.

Still, Jennifer knew that she had a lot of work ahead of her. "This is someone who's fresh in the public's mind. So you need to do your homework on this gig," she commented. Jennifer studied Selena's singing, dancing, and mannerisms. She watched videos of Selena every night to learn her moves and singing style, even though executives had decided that Jennifer should lip synch to Selena's real voice. The actress totally immersed herself in learning all about the slain star.

Jennifer even moved in with the Quintanilla family for a while, saying, "I tried to forget about my own mannerisms in order to pick up Selena's. I learned how to dance like she did. To laugh like she did. To imitate her sense of humor. I walked through the streets of Corpus Christi [Texas, Selena's hometown] soaking up the atmosphere. Trying to feel like a Tejana." Selena's family began to notice the similarities between their daughter and Jennifer. "You never eat, you never drink enough water. . . . You're just like Selena!" Mrs. Quintanilla joked.

In fact, Selena claimed she liked to keep her figure by eating pizza. While Jennifer's figure was curvaceous just like Selena's, the actress still had to pad her backside for the part. Jennifer also wore a wig. The makeup department even considered fitting Jennifer with a prosthetic nose that looked more like Selena's. But the fake rubber nose was fairly obvious in screen tests and they eventually decided to go without it. "One of the things that made her so popular was that she was always just herself. She didn't try to hide her figure, all that stuff," Jennifer explained. "She was Latin, she had dark hair, and she dyed her hair even blacker than it was. She wore bright red lipstick. It was never her thing to say, 'Maybe I won't wear this miniskirt, maybe my butt won't look so big if I wear this instead.' She accentuated what she had," Jennifer claimed. "And women look up to her and say, 'My body's just like that. She's just showing it, so why should I feel ashamed of it?'"

Thrilled with the opportunity to play Selena, Jennifer had to temporarily put her preparations on hold. She journeyed to the Amazon to film another movie—the thriller *Anaconda*. She played Terri Flores, a first-time director who is making a documentary film about the anaconda-worshipping Sirishama Indian tribe.

The role was intensely physical, and Jennifer enjoyed doing her own stunt work. "I'm tough that way," she said. "I'll do anything." The physical demands of the part did have a downside, however: "They have pictures of me doing the fittings at night for Selena while I was filming [the few Los Angeles scenes of] *Anaconda*. I was like the Elephant Woman from the hips down. It was a major bruise movie."

Jennifer also made a new friend on the set. She and rapper Ice Cube clicked from the start. The two talked about music and L.A. They both were wary of life in the jungle and wanted to get back to the concrete and high-rises of the city. Jennifer soon got her wish, returning to work on the set of *Selena*.

The film was shot in four months on location in Mexico and Texas. Selena's parents were on the set as advisors, and Jennifer felt a duty to them. The actress remembered the emotions on the set. "Selena's family was right there, and they were so involved with the whole movie. I became the focal point of all this energy: good energy, sad energy, everything. A lot of nights I went home and I just felt so drained, so tired, so sad."

However, Jennifer was at work every morning, ready to be Selena. She became so involved in the character that by the end of filming, Jennifer said she could look in the mirror and see Selena in her. While she was working, Jennifer tried not to think about the story's sad ending. She claimed that one of the hardest things about playing Selena was remembering the young singer did not know she was going to die. Instead, Jennifer portrayed the fun-loving, prank-playing Selena. Jennifer said she never cried—until she saw the film's rough cut.

"Everyone who had seen it kept telling me how they cried while watching it. So here I am, and it's getting close to the end, and I'm still not crying. All of a sudden they get to this one scene, after Selena passes away, and I just broke down. I was sobbing uncontrollably for about a half-hour, forty-five minutes. I needed to cry for her, but I didn't expect such a reaction," Jennifer confessed.

Luckily, Jennifer had Ojani to turn to for support. The two were getting serious, but Jennifer was still surprised by his proposal at the *Selena* wrap party in late 1996. "All of a sudden Ojani takes the mike, and I'm thinking he's going to say something about how hard I worked. He comes up to my table and in Spanish he says, 'I just want to say one thing: Jennifer, will you marry me?'" A stunned Jennifer accepted. "Everybody just burst out into applause. I started crying. Then he gets

When Ojani Noa pro-posed marriage at the Selena *wrap party, Jennifer immediately accepted. The newly-weds are shown here arriving at the premiere of* Anaconda *in April 1997, less than two months after their wedding.*

down on one knee and puts the ring on my finger. It was very, very romantic," she recalled. Neither one of them wanted to wait very long, so that night, they chose February 22 as their wedding date and were married before 200 friends and family members just weeks before the *Selena* premiere.

Selena opened in March 1997, and Jennifer quickly became a star. The 26-year-old felt as though her life couldn't get any better. She had a loving family, a supportive husband, and a blossoming career. *People* magazine included her in their "Young & Hot: 30 Under 30" article. She was also grateful that the film she worked so

After the release of Selena, Jennifer received a great deal of recognition and many prestigious awards, including ALMA's Best Actress Award, which recognizes Latino contributions to the television and movie industry.

hard on was being well received by the public. "This is not only a wonderful role for me, but it is a wonderful opportunity for all Latin people," Jennifer told reporters after the film's release. "We have this big-budget Latin movie with a Latin cast about a Latin family made by a huge Hollywood studio. This is a great moment for the Latin people and for all Latin actors. By the same token, the only reason we're doing this movie is that someone very special was murdered."

To many people, Jennifer became known as the actress who played Selena. "One of my friends, also an actress, told me after she had seen the movie, 'It doesn't matter what comes next in your career, you will always have this.' That is how I look at it. I worked hard, it came out very well and the public will remember that

I played the role well, and that is why I consider it a positive thing."

The movie was also positively received by many awards committees. *Selena* won four awards at the 1998 American Latino Media Arts Awards (ALMAs), for Best Film, Best Actress for Jennifer, Best Actor for Edward James Olmos, and Best Director for Gregory Nava. Jennifer also took home the evening's Lasting Image Award. At the Lone Star Film and Television Awards, she won Best Actress. In the same year, she also received a Golden Globe nomination for Best Actress and an MTV Movie Award nomination for Best Breakthrough Performance.

With the acclaim and awards came the realization that Jennifer was now a role model as well as a celebrity. She was constantly spotted and approached by fans. "When I first became well-known, I was freaking about it. Edward James Olmos once sat me down and said, 'You are very important to your community.' The room started spinning. I was like, I cannot take all this responsibility on my shoulders. I'm one little person!"

Jennifer knew that there was no turning back. After all, this is what she wanted, and she had to believe she could handle what lay ahead.

5

AN OUT-OF-SIGHT CAREER

"I think *Selena* really got my name out there, but Jennifer Lopez didn't do a bad job of that, either," Jennifer boasted in 1997.

The actress had reason to feel successful. Before the premiere of *Selena*, she was hard at work on the set of her next film, *U-Turn*, with high-powered director Oliver Stone. The director had chosen Jennifer over Caucasian actress Sharon Stone to play incest victim Grace McKenna. He had to beg her to take the part because years earlier Jennifer had walked out of an audition with Stone. Instead of paying attention to Jennifer during her monologue, the director had straightened up his office. After several apologies from Stone, Jennifer was happy to work with the director whom she called "a genius." She explained, "I love Oliver, loved working with him. He was totally great to me—a real actor's director." Because of Jennifer's commitment to other projects, the director even rearranged the film's production schedule to accommodate her. The director felt Jennifer's attitude and work ethic were worth the extra effort. "She's a tough chick. She was barefoot for days with fake blood on

---

Her career still on the rise, Jennifer starred with veteran actor Sean Penn in Oliver Stone's 1997 film, U-Turn, *which also featured Billy Bob Thornton, Nick Nolte, and Jon Voight.*

her," Stone later recalled.

Besides a talented director, Jennifer was also set to work with an accomplished cast, including Sean Penn, Billy Bob Thornton, Nick Nolte, Jon Voight, Joaquin Phoenix, and Claire Danes. The story is about Jennifer's character, Grace McKenna—an Apache Indian who, although married to one of the most powerful men in the small town of Superior, Arizona, is desperately unhappy. She tries to convince a gambler named Bobby Cooper (Sean Penn), who is passing through town on his way to Las Vegas to pay off a debt, to help her escape. Cooper gets involved in the lives of the town's citizens when Grace's husband offers him money to kill his wife, and Grace, in turn, offers Cooper money to murder her husband.

Like Selena, the role of Grace McKenna was intense. But unlike Selena, who had lived the American Dream until her murder, Grace's closet was full of skeletons. Jennifer found herself panicking about how to understand an incest victim. "I have the most wonderful father, you-know-what-I-mean? I didn't want to think about fathers molesting their daughters or killing their wives," she told *Vibe* magazine. "I had to call my acting coach and he faxed me this article on Meryl Streep, where she was talking about going to difficult places. It's about not being afraid to go there. And at the end of the day it's a job. I'm getting paid to go there," Jennifer rationalized.

The end result was a promising piece of acting by Jennifer. Unfortunately, the film was panned by critics. "The first two-thirds of *U-Turn* is a rude, seductive head bender," wrote *Entertainment Weekly*. "But around the time it turns from day to night, the film begins to lose its tricky aura of borderline surreal mystery. It becomes another rigged, what-will-happen-next suspense game, and you begin to sense just how arbitrary the twists are." Jennifer was getting a reputation as an actress who starred in bad films with great casts and powerful directors. But her talent and popularity were undeniable. Jennifer felt that 1997 had been a banner year, both personally and professionally.

Next, she was paired with heartthrob George Clooney, star of the TV series *ER*, in 1998's *Out of Sight*. While filming the action flick, she also presented at the Academy Awards and did a photo shoot for the cover of *Vanity Fair*'s Hollywood issue. Whenever she was in front of the camera, Jennifer was ready to work. She was also ready to get paid some serious money. Her asking price had doubled in just one year—since *Selena*—to $2 million.

Jennifer's role of Karen Sisco in *Out of Sight* was also not written for a Latina actress. Director Steven Soderbergh originally thought of Sandra Bullock of *Speed* for the part. He changed his mind once he saw Jennifer's reading. The actress read a scene in which she and Clooney are stuck in the trunk of a car. Soderbergh knew the chemistry between the two was magical, and he claimed George was better with Jennifer than any of the other actresses. He felt Jennifer also did a great job of playing both sweet and tough, the two qualities of the federal marshal out to nab Clooney's bank robber character, Jack Foley.

"It's not a question of, are people ready to see a Latina actress in big movies," Soderbergh said. "The point is, people are ready to see *Jennifer* in high-profile movies. She's sexy, intelligent, beautiful but not implausibly beautiful, and she's got really good instincts and very good technical chops, which is rare." Jennifer was thrilled by the compliment. "When Hollywood starts considering me for roles where ethnic background doesn't matter, that's an even bigger step in the right direction for me."

The role was the right step in her career as well, because *Out of Sight* is critically regarded as Jennifer's best film to date. The film is a blend of action, romance, suspense, and drama which follows the escape of prisoner Jack Foley. Sisco is present for the escape; she gets kidnapped and locked in the trunk of Foley's car. When she's released, she hunts Foley down, in part because it's her job, but also because she is attracted to him.

It was easy for Jennifer to feel attracted to her costar. Besides their natural chemistry onscreen, Jennifer and George got along like old friends once the cameras stopped rolling. "We were talking about close-ups and how the star is always first. So on the set we were fighting, 'No, no, you go first.' 'No, *you* go first.' We were both so used to not being first," Jennifer explained.

Even though the premiere of the film in June 1998 should have been a joyful occasion for Jennifer, she was too upset about her personal life to enjoy the audience's positive response. She and Ojani had only been married for a year but had been having problems almost from the start. Once again, Jennifer's career and ambition seemed to be the forces behind the split. "She wanted her career," Ojani said. Jennifer thought Ojani would understand the demands of her work schedule. "Many people criticized me for getting married so quickly. It's hard for such a macho man to accept that his wife earns more money than he does, that she

Jennifer felt completely at ease with Out of Sight *costar George Clooney. They had a natural chemistry together in front of the camera and acted like old friends between the shooting of their scenes.*

wears sexy clothing, and that she does love scenes in films." Despite the end of their marriage, the two remain good friends. Ojani now manages the Conga Room, a Latin club and restaurant, which Jennifer co-owns with actor Jimmy Smits and comedian Paul Rodriguez.

Looking back on her marriage, Jennifer said: "I've learned that marriage isn't just about love. I was young and naive and thought that love conquered the world—but you have to compromise to a certain extent. Sometimes people are just not ready to do that at that point in their lives." However, the self-proclaimed "seeker of

Since her divorce, Jennifer has been linked romantically with many men, including Sean "Puffy" Combs. "My personal life has to remain just that, personal," she said in response to such rumors.

love" hasn't given up on having both a family and a career. She has been linked to many men, including Sony executive Tommy Mottola, Latin singer Marc Anthony, boxer Oscar de la Hoya, and music star Sean "Puffy" Combs (a.k.a. Puff Daddy).

Rumors about Jennifer and Sean Combs escalated after gunfire erupted in a Times Square nightclub on December 27, 1999. The two fled the scene in the rear seat of a 1999 Lincoln Navigator, which was pulled over by police after running several red lights. Police reportedly found an allegedly stolen 9-mm pistol on the floor of the front seat and arrested everyone in the vehicle. After being held for more than 10 hours, handcuffed to a bench, Jennifer was released, and prosecutors dropped all charges against her. Combs, who repeatedly claimed his innocence, was charged with criminal possession of a weapon and possession of stolen property.

While speculation about Jennifer's social life continues, she remains mysterious, saying, "My personal life has to remain just that, personal."

Jennifer did, however, reveal to *Cosmopolitan* magazine that she plans to work hard for the next couple of years and then settle down with a husband and children, in a big house in Miami. "I'm going to have it all. Everything. Why not?"

6

ACTRESS/SINGER/DANCER

After the release of *Out of Sight*, Jennifer took a short break from films to concentrate on her album. But she couldn't resist lending her vocal talents to another project as well. She voiced the character of a worker ant named Azteca in the animated DreamWorks' film *Antz*. Jennifer enjoyed working on the family film alongside other Hollywood heavyweights, including Woody Allen, Sylvester Stallone, and Anne Bancroft. "Animation is really fun. There are no set rules and you can just go for different things. It's a totally different type of acting." Besides recording, Jennifer was also doing some product endorsements, filming commercials for L'Oreal hair coloring and cosmetics.

After the success of *On the 6*, Jennifer is contemplating a tour. She is also reading through scripts and deciding on her next film projects. First up is another thriller called *The Cell*, in which she plays a scientist who uses a revolutionary medical technique to invade the mind of a comatose serial killer in order to save a kidnap victim. Industry papers also linked the actress to the film *Angel Eyes*, about a cop reeling from an abusive childhood; a

---

Like her role model Rita Moreno, Jennifer is recognized as a talented actress, singer, and dancer. Her hometown, New York City, honored her as grand marshal of the May 1999 National Puerto Rican Day Parade.

remake of *A Star Is Born* with Will Smith; and the romantic comedy *The Wedding Planner*, costarring Brendan Fraser. No matter which she chooses, she'll be very well paid for her work. Jennifer currently makes at least $5 million per picture.

At the end of a long day, Jennifer hops into her Mercedes convertible and heads home to her West Hollywood apartment to relax. Her favorite room is her bedroom, which is all-white and draped in gauze. Besides shopping for expensive designer clothes by Prada and Valentino and getting stopped on the street for autographs, Jennifer claims her everyday life is no different than most. She says it's a big night if she and her girlfriends go out to dinner.

If she does find the time for a night of dancing, Jennifer usually gets interrupted by her cell phone, which she claims is permanently attached to her ear. Usually, she's on the phone with her manager scheduling an interview. "When I first started doing television years ago, it was like nobody cared. I was very open and free. Then you become famous and people care about every little thing you do, every aspect of your life. They become intrigued, I guess. . . . They want to know who you are. It's flattering at first . . ."

Jennifer learned the hard way about watching what she says in one-on-one chats with reporters. During an interview with *Movieline*, she made the mistake of insulting several fellow actors, while she herself endured press assertions that her costars found her difficult. Later, Jennifer and fellow Latina actress Salma Hayek traded barbs after Jennifer accused Salma of lying about being asked to star in *Selena*.

The actress has also been told she's overly

ambitious. "Is [ambition] like a bad thing with women?" Jennifer has asked.

She went on to explain:

> I'm ambitious, but so is everybody—men, women. Where I come from, if you see somebody who stays home, it's like that's dirty too. I want something, you want something; you should do whatever makes you happy. If going after things and accomplishing things makes you happy, then fine. If staying home and babysitting makes you happy, that's cool.

The result of her ambition and the insults is that she has been branded a diva, which makes her uncomfortable. "I have a problem with the term," she explained to *Entertainment Weekly*. "I feel like it means that you are mean to people, that you look down on people, and I'm not that type of person." She said, "I don't try to be nice. I don't try to not be nice."

Diva or not, one thing there's no denying is Jennifer's good looks. Named to *People* magazine's famous "50 Most Beautiful People" list in 1997 and 1999, Jennifer claims her dad is the one who makes her feel the most attractive. "Every time I call [home], my dad says, 'Hi, gorgeous.'"

In the competitive world of Hollywood, staying beautiful is a full-time job. Jennifer likes to visit spas: "I do the scrubs, the baths, the massage, the facial—everything." She also works out up to four times a week and watches what she eats. "I'll have egg whites in the morning, carbs for lunch, and a salad for dinner. I don't like nasty food—stuff that's really greasy," she asserted. When she does indulge, Jennifer likes "[c]ookies with coffee—

Jennifer's success and popularity has been noticed by the mainstream media. In addition to acting, recording, and touring, she is in high demand for television talk shows. On The Oprah Winfrey Show, *she appeared with host Winfrey (right) and fellow Latino star Ricky Martin (left).*

that makes me feel good." She prefers to wear just a little makeup with a shiny lip gloss. To stay grounded, Jennifer likes to meditate and reported, "I do light meditation to calm myself down when I'm anxious, breathing exercises and stuff like that."

Despite all of her efforts to stay slim, Jennifer often gets grouped with larger women in Hollywood, even though she's 5' 6" and a healthy 120 pounds. "But I don't take it as an insult, because they're identifying me as a real person. If that helps other people's self-esteem, good! It helps mine too!" Still, her round backside is the focus of much conversation—cameramen have even fought to photograph her from behind. She thinks the subject is tired and wishes everyone would stop talking about her famous derriere.

When the pressure gets to be too much, Jennifer likes to head for the East Coast. "I feel like I'm the same simple girl from The Bronx," she told *People*. Her parents still live in the neighborhood where Jennifer grew up, and both of her sisters live in nearby Manhattan.

Jennifer returned home to play grand marshal in the city's Puerto Rican Day Parade in May 1999. She also visited some nearby schools to answer questions and tell the kids to stay in school and get an education. She told them not to fear failure in pursuit of their dreams. After all, she reminded them, if she had taken the negative comments to heart, she wouldn't be where she is today.

"I don't really concentrate on negative things, especially when it comes to my career," she told *Sony Style*. "If somebody picks up a paint brush, they don't go, 'What if this painting turns out ugly?' You get up and start painting whether people like it or not. . . . I just try to do the best work I can and work as hard as I can at it."

Jennifer Lopez is a gifted and versatile performer who plans to keep entertaining her fans and hopes to make some new ones. "I consider myself a complete actress. I dance, I act, I sing. . . . I don't want to do just one thing. I want to do it all," Jennifer said. "I wouldn't feel right if I didn't do it. I think I have much more to offer. I would feel bad if I reached the age of sixty and thought about what I should have done." Instead, Jennifer knows her future will be filled to the brim with plenty of each of her passions. "When I look to the future, I don't see the pinnacle of what I'll reach, I see this endless hallway."

CHRONOLOGY

1970   Born on July 24 to David and Guadalupe Lopez in The Bronx, New York.

1977   Begins dance classes.

1987   Graduates from high school and decides to become a dancer.

1988   Tours with *Golden Musicals of Broadway* and *Synchronicity*.

1991   Is picked to be a Fly Girl on FOX-TV's *In Living Color*.

1993   Appears on series *Second Chances*.

1994   Stars in series *South Central*.

1995   Appears in series *Hotel Malibu* and made-for-television film *Nurses on the Line: The Crash of Flight 7*; makes big screen debut in Gregory Nava's *My Family/Mi Familia*; films *The Money Train*.

1996   Costars in *Jack* with Robin Williams.

1997   Marries Ojani Noa; *Blood and Wine* is released; *Selena* is released; stars in *Anaconda*; *U-Turn* is released.

1998   Divorces Ojani Noa; stars in *Out of Sight* with George Clooney; signs endorsement deals with L'Oreal and Coca-Cola; lends vocal talents to role of Azteca in animated feature *Antz*.

1999   Releases debut album, *On the 6*, which goes platinum; films *The Cell*.

ACCOMPLISHMENTS

Television

1991–93   *In Living Color* (series)

1993–94   *Second Chances* (series)

1994   *South Central* (series)
              Hotel Malibu (series)

1995   *Nurses on the Line: The Crash of Flight 7* (TV movie)

Filmography

1995   *My Family/Mi Familia*
              The Money Train

1996   *Jack*

1997   *Blood and Wine*
              Selena
              Anaconda
              U-Turn

1998   *Out of Sight*
              Antz (voice)

2000   *The Cell*

Discography

1999   *On the 6*

Awards (Acting)

1998   ALMA for Best Actress and Lasting Image Award for *Selena*
              Lone Star Film & Television Award for Best Actress for *Selena*

Awards (Music)

1999   Teen Choice Award for Song of the Summer—"If You Had My Love"

FURTHER READING

Duncan, Patricia J. *Jennifer Lopez: An Unauthorized Biography*. New York: St. Martins Press, 1999.

Farley, Christopher John. "Latin Music Pops." *Time*, May 24, 1999.

France, Bill. "Out of Sight." *Elle*, July 1999.

Frankel, Martha. "Jennifer Lopez Loves To . . ." *Cosmopolitan*, March 1999.

Hadley-Garcia, George. *Hispanic Hollywood: The Latins in Motion Pictures*. Secaucus, N.J.: Citadel Press, 1991.

Hensley, Dennis. "How Do You Say 'Hot' in Spanish?" *Cosmopolitan*, April 1997.

Hoskyns, Barney. "Selena." *Interview*, April 1997.

Mitchell, Wendy. "Jennifer Lopez." *Sony Style*, Fall 1999.

Pener, Degen. "From Here to Divinity." *Entertainment Weekly*, Oct. 9, 1998.

Smith, Kyle. "Shaking It Up." *People*, Sept. 13, 1999.

ABOUT THE AUTHOR

ANNE E. HILL has been writing for kids and young adults since she was in her teens. Her first article was published in a teen magazine at age 16. Since then, she graduated Magna Cum Laude with a B.A. in English from Franklin and Marshall College, where she was a member of Phi Beta Kappa and wrote for the *Franklin and Marshall Magazine*. She is the author of *Denzel Washington*, which was named one of the New York Public Library's Best Books for Teenagers; *Ekaterina Gordeeva*; *Female Firsts in Their Fields: Broadcasting and Journalism*; *Cameron Diaz*; and the forthcoming titles *Sergei Grinkov* and *Sandra Bullock*. Mrs. Hill is also a writer for the Concert Connection's All Star Teen Line. She lives in Wayne, Pennsylvania, with her husband, George.

INDEX